Arts & Health
Activity Book for Kids

Shanda Palsulich

12 Weeks of activities for kids 6-12 that will encourage healthy habits while engaging their inner artist

Front and back cover photographs from Shutterstock artist SewCream.
Christmas image from Shutterstock artist Sandra Cunningham.
Ripe tomatoes image from Shutterstock artist Fotokostic.
Sunset river image from Shutterstock artist TSN52.
Cows grazing image from Shutterstock artist Przemek Iciak.
Chicken sunset image from Shutterstock artist Moonborne.
Bowl of berries image from Shutterstock artist Goskova Tatiana.
Heart fruit bowl image from Shutterstock artist Rob Hainer.
Sample project images taken by Shanda Palsulich,
Sample artwork contributed by Alyse Palsulich, Mark Palsulich, and Shanda Palsulich

ISBN: Print 978-0-578-84306-3

CONTENTS

This book is dedicated to my husband David and children Alyse, Luke, Mark, & Michael.

INTRODUCTION

I wrote this book out of my love for two areas, nutrition and education (using fun and effective teaching methods-specifically the arts). It is my hope that through the reading of my stories you will think about your own stories. While learning the educational nutritional information, I encourage you to think of ways to incorporate healthy habits into your own life. As you are integrating what you are learning into beautiful works of art, I want you to have fun while gaining an understanding of the material. I also hope this book will open up different art mediums to you that you can use for fun or for any type of learning you do in the future. Integrating learning with art takes the learning to a deeper level of understanding that you will be more likely to remember. Lastly, I hope you share the beauty you create with other people. If you can, do this with one or more other people. You can build a community of family and/or friends to experience greater health and have fun while doing it.

This book is written with six sections. You can take as much time to work through the sections as you like. But, they should be completed in order.

Shanda ♥

 # YOUR STORY

Supplies: ❏ Favorite writing pen(s) ❏ Paper ❏ Colored pencils or crayons or markers	Time to Complete: 1~2 Weeks

MY HALLOWEEN EXPERIENCE

My little brother and I hurried to get on our homemade costumes. Once I dressed up as a bag of jelly beans. I was surrounded by a clear garbage bag filled with colorful balloons and pretty tights on my legs. My mom was so creative without the help of Pinterest! Our grandmothers and great-grandmother lived very far from one another, sadly all our grandfathers had passed too early. We started with my great-grandma's little pink house set out in the middle of nowhere. I loved going down the hill and over the little bump that made my stomach flip. She always made delicious popcorn balls. They were my favorite Halloween treat. Then we would drive about 30 minutes to my grandma's house where she would give us goody bags filled with treats. My mom would spend what felt like forever visiting with each of the grandmas before moving on to the next. When we returned home, we were allowed to go up and down our own street, but that was all. My parents believed you should only go to your own neighborhood for trick-or-treating.

MAP OF HALLOWEEN ROUTE²

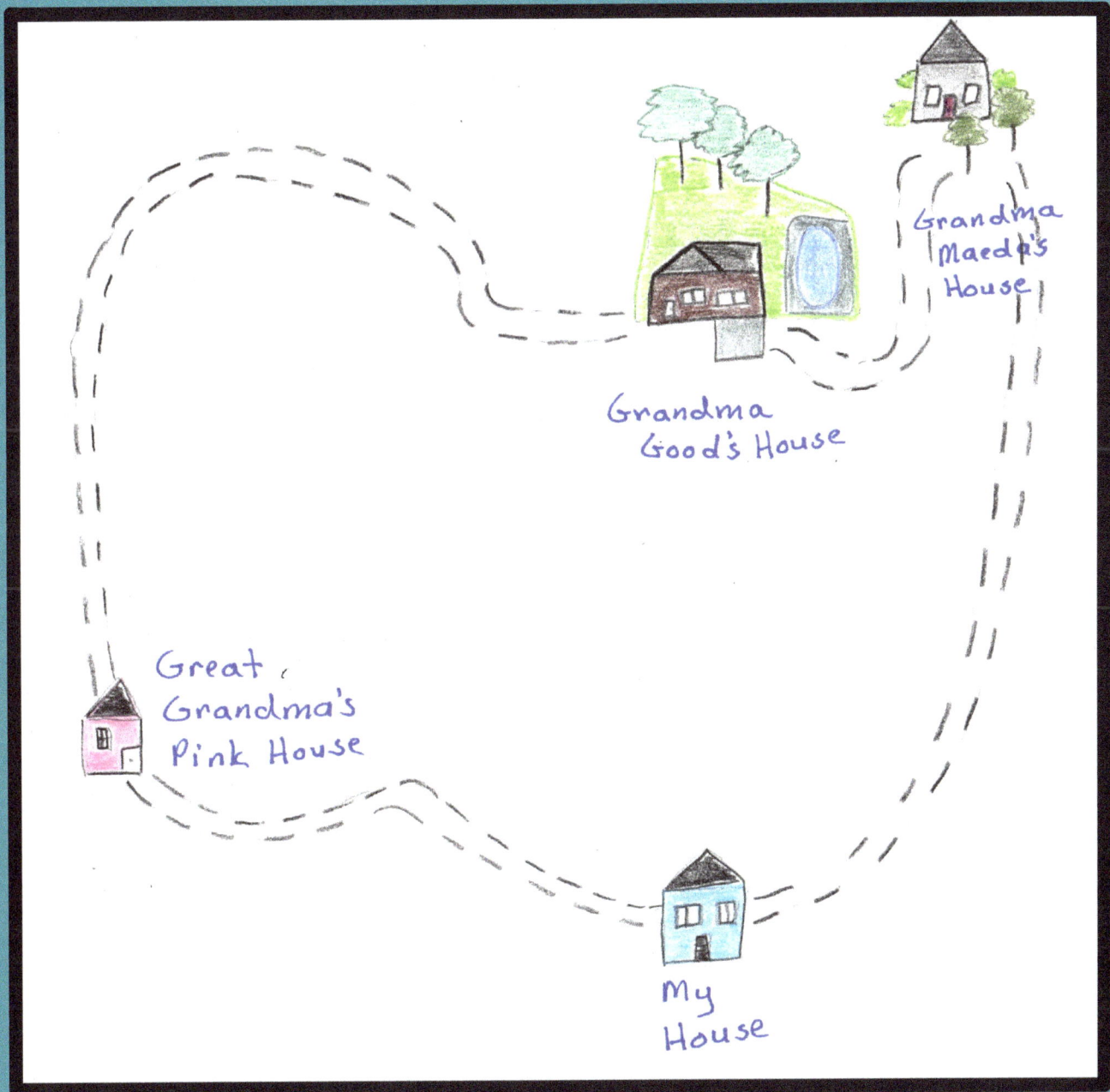

Grandma Maeda's House

Grandma Good's House

Great Grandma's Pink House

My House

ACTIVITY

We all have a story and that story makes up our culture. Our experiences, routines, religion, foods, traditions, even the way we decorate our homes makes up our own individual culture. Food plays a large part of our celebrations. Those times of celebration are usually fun and exciting. We often take the time to slowly eat and enjoy that time with family and friends. This is a very healthy way to eat. Sharing a meal with the people we love, taking the time to eat slowly, and having gratitude for the food and people puts our bodies and minds into a parasympathetic state. This is the state where we will produce the enzymes needed to digest our foods and our bodies will most easily absorb the nutrients. It is a healthy way to eat for our minds and our bodies.

Think back to some of your favorite family celebrations. Make a list below:

_____

_____

_____

_____

_____

You are going to tell your own story. Pick one or two of the celebrations to write about. Think about the following questions while writing: What did you do? Who was it with? How did you feel? What kind of food did you eat? What did you love about it? Was it connected to a religious celebration? Write out a rough draft of your story on your own paper. If you need to, ask a family member or friend to help you with some of the details. You might want to look through pictures of your event to trigger your memories.

Work on your story until it is just how you want it and then use your best handwriting to write it out on the next page.

FAMILY   CELEBRATIONS   HOLIDAYS
LAUGHTER   FRIENDS
FOOD   FUN

YOUR STORY

YOUR STORY MAP

Now draw a story map. You can make this as detailed as you want. Think about the following questions: Where did your event happen? What buildings or structures do you remember? What were the colors you saw? Map out your story so that someone could follow along as you shared it with them. You can be as detailed as you want. Once you have made your map, make sure to color it. Attach it below.

REFLECTION

What is your favorite food that you eat at this event? Locate that recipe and attach it below. Make this recipe with another person and take a picture. Attach your picture.

RECIPE

PICTURE

Now it is time for you to share your story with another person. Remember, this is your story, you can be proud of your story and your traditions and your culture. It is part of what makes you YOU! Ask them to share their favorite traditions and foods with you.

★   Who did you share your story with?

★   What was their response?

★   What did you like most about their story?

★   You can always add to your story and integrate other cultural practices if you want. Are there any traditions you would like to add to your own?

★   What will you remember from this activity?

MY CHRISTMAS MEMORIES

The thrill of the Christmas season filled me with excitement. My cousins would come from out of town and stay for a week. Every night we would eat delicious Japanese food prepared by my aunts and grandma, who was raised in Japan and later moved to the states. Everyone loved the meals. Then the table would be cleared, the dishes washed and the cards and coins came out. The kids played in a separate room from the adults, and used buttons instead of real money. The game was called Shanghai. It was a card game with several rounds that progressively got harder. There was much laughter with a little bit of playful bickering.

Christmas Eve was the most special of the evenings. After the dishes were cleaned and ALL the family pictures were taken we would take turns opening gifts. It started with the youngest and progressed until it was my turn and then we would start again. After the gifts were opened we would play Shanghai. It was a late night filled with fun, treats, gifts, and laughter.

Christmas morning my brother and I would wake to stockings brimming with gifts and wrapped presents under the tree that were left by Santa. After we opened the gifts and got ready we would pack up and go to my grandmother's house on my mom's side. My Grandma Good made stockings for all the kids and adults. My favorite stocking treats were the chocolate covered orange jelly sticks and the peanut clusters. We would sit around the table and eat a delicious meal with turkey, oyster stuffing, and sparkling cider. The rest of the day would be spent playing games, laughing, and eating treats.

On the drive home in the dark, the lights would illuminate from the depths of the snow on the bushes. Due to the heat of the lights, they would sink into the bushes of snow and glow red, green, yellow, blue, and orange. I loved looking through the icicles hanging from the roof eaves over the windows to the gathered families and lit Christmas trees. Once home, I would fall into bed, exhausted.

WATER

Water is vital for life. It surrounds us and is in us. My Grandma Good had an underground swimming pool that I loved to swim in when I was a little girl. I remember many summer days of swimming with my mom and friends. The shock of the cool water when I first dove into the pool was exhilarating. The water felt silky as it glided over my skin. The shimmer of the sun reflecting off the surface of the pool water was beautiful. I also enjoy the fresh smell of the rain and the crash of ocean waves. I am mesmerized by the deep blue of a glacier and the rushing waters of a river. I love water. It is one of the most beautiful parts of nature.

Water is also essential for life. Our bodies need water every day to help nutrients to pass around our bodies. It brings the good nutrition into our cells and takes away the waste that we excrete. Without enough water we can suffer painful kidney stones, get headaches, body aches, fatigue, anxiety, depression, irritability, and more. You should try to drink your water throughout the day. In the morning, fill up your water bottle and make it a habit to sip throughout the day. Your brain and body will function better.

ACTIVITY

Think of your favorite times related to water such as walking in the rain, sledding down a snow hill, fishing on a lake, or looking at the early morning frost on the tips of the bare trees. It can be anything related to water.

List them below:

_____

_____

_____

_____

_____

Get out your watercolor paints and create a picture of that scene. As you are working, think about all the ways that water nourishes your body and the planet around you. Try mixing your paint to create different shades of colors.

When you are finished with your painting, write a poem about your water scene or the role of water in the body or in nature. It could be a definition poem, a color poem, a place poem, a list poem, an ode poem, or any type of poem inspired by your art.

Ripples of Water

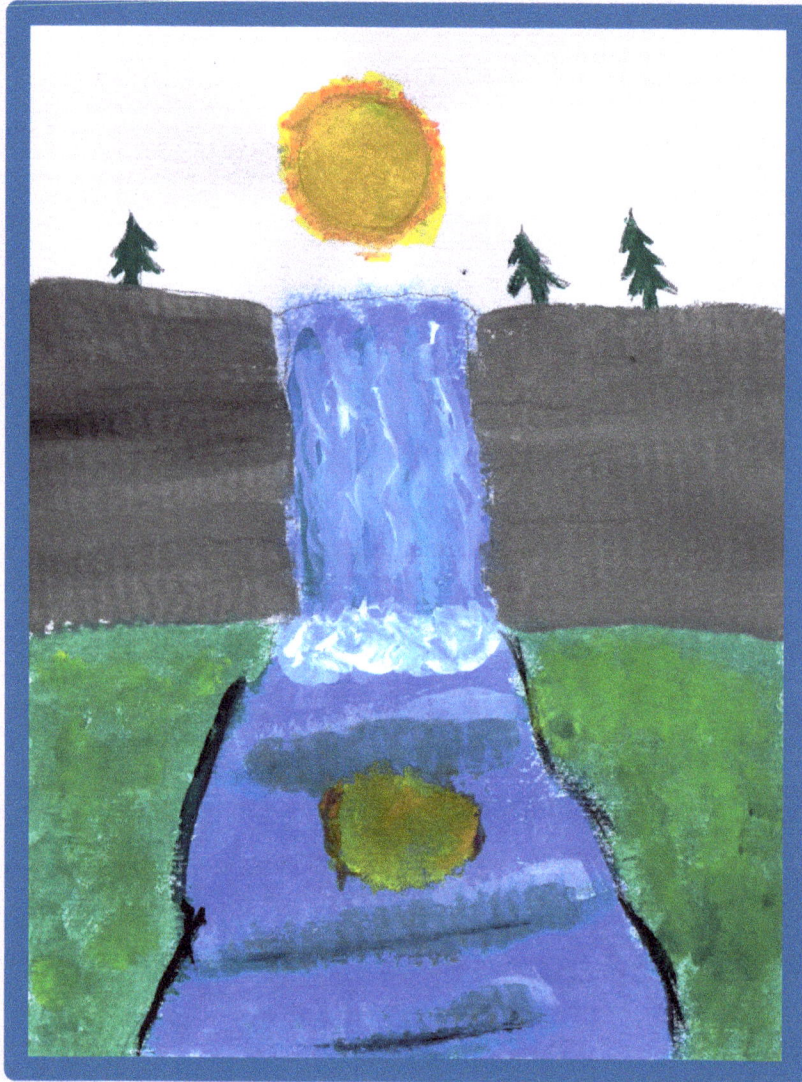

Ripples reflect
beams of light,

In a lake ever so
calm.

The sun watches
day turn to night,

As the water
sustains our home.

~Alyse

WATER

Drips from the sky.

Flows over the rocks.

Rushes to the shore.

Brings life to the cell.

Removes waste from
the body.

Freezes into unique
beautiful crystals.

Home to many.

Upholder of life.

Attach Your Painting

Write or Attach Your Poem

REFLECTION

★ How does your scene make you feel?

★ When was the last time you had this experience with water?

★ Why did you pick the colors you did?

★ Did you mix your paints to create different shades?

★ Thinking about your own health and how much water you drink, do you drink water throughout the day?

★ What are you going to do to ensure you are drinking enough water?

★ Reflect back to the last lesson. Have you taken the time to eat slowly, enjoy your meals, and have gratitude?

*Remember, eating slowly with gratitude and in a relaxed state prepares your body and mind for proper digestion.

Spend some time outside enjoying the fresh air, beautiful greenery, and a water feature like a river, waterfall, pond, the ocean, or a lake. Watch and listen to the water. It does not just nourish our bodies, it is calming to our soul. It rejuvenates us when we spend time in nature.

CARB♥HYDRATES

Supplies:	Time to Complete:

❏ Food Art
   ❏ Variety of fruits
   ❏ Variety of vegetables
❏ Food Mosaic
   ❏ White glue
   ❏ Scissors
   ❏ Black permanent marker
   ❏ Cardboard square
   ❏ Magazines or card stock
	2 Weeks

As a child my mom and I would plant a small garden. I loved when the cherry tomatoes would ripen and I could pop a warm sun-ripened tomato into my mouth. It was like finding little presents when I would discover a vegetable that was hidden beneath the foliage.

My grandma had a large garden and many fruit trees. It was such a joy to visit and get to eat Japanese pears and peaches right off the tree. She also grew strawberries, cucumbers, tomatoes, peas, and more. She was generous and shared her produce with our family all summer. She really had a green thumb. Her family room was filled with beautiful flowers too. I was fortunate to have such delicious produce as a child.

I did not know as a child how good for my body all the organic sun-ripened produce was. It was grown without chemicals being used to keep away predators. Unlike the produce from the store that is picked unripe and shipped hundreds of miles, it was picked at the peak of ripeness. Today, I do not have a garden space, but I look for the best looking organic produce in the stores and from farmer's markets.

The greater the variety of color the more nutrients my body is receiving. Vegetables are a source of carbohydrates that provide not only energy, but all sorts of vitamins, minerals, and fiber that our bodies need. Oranges have vitamin C, bananas have potassium, avocados and broccoli have fiber. These different nutrients serve many purposes in our bodies like helping our immune system and transporting ions into our cells for proper functioning. Fiber scrubs our intestines and keeps everything running smoothly. It is important for us to eat a wide variety of fruits and vegetables each day.

ACTIVITY

Create two works of art using fruits and vegetables. Get as much variety as you can. Take pictures before enjoying the "fruits" of your labor with friends and/or family. Here are some examples.

A
T
T
A
C
H

T
H
E

P
I
C
T
U
R
E
S

H
E
R
E

G
R
E
A
T

J
O
B

Extend Your Knowledge

List the fruits and vegetable you used in your work of art in the table below. Then look up the main vitamins and/or minerals they contain and how they are important for the body and put that in the table too.

Fruit or Vegetable	Vitamins and/or Minerals	Main Function in the Body

ACTIVITY

Choose your favorite fruit or vegetable and follow along with the steps and pictures below to create a beautiful mosaic picture.

1-Measure a square or rectangle on cardboard or a file folder for the base

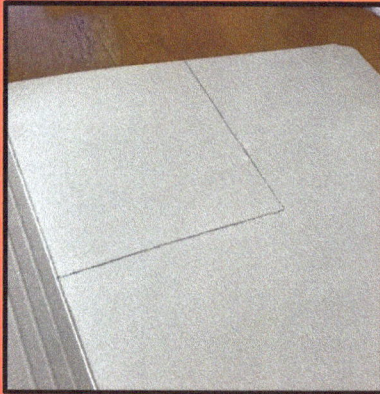

2-Cut out the base

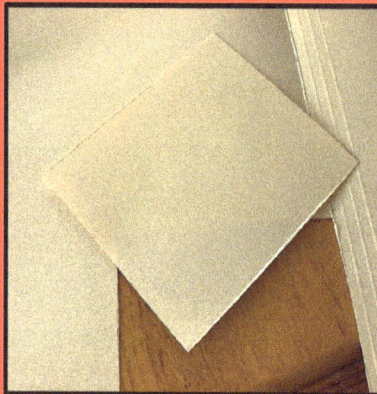

3-Draw your shape with a pencil and trace with a permanent marker

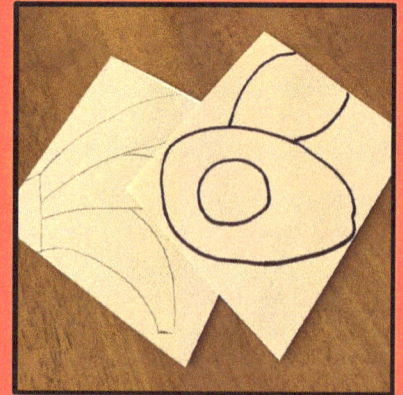

4-Select the colored paper you want from magazines or cardstock

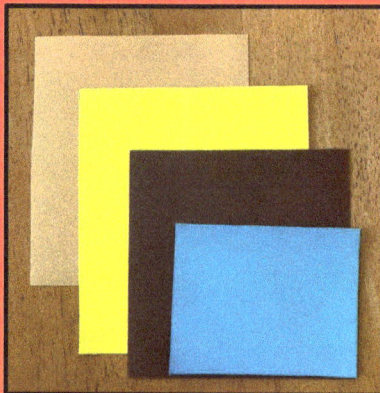

5-Cut out strips and then cut the strips into little squares or rectangles

6-Rub white glue over a small area and start placing the colored paper

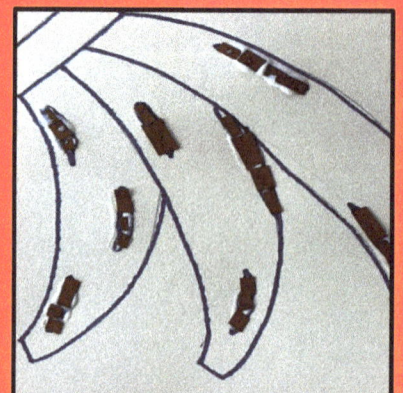

ACTIVITY

7-Continue adding colored squares/rectangles until the shape is completely filled

8-Add a colorful background to fill in all of the base and add a border to make your finished product really stand out

★ What is the most interesting thing you learned about carbohydrates?

★ What is your favorite fruit?

★ What is your favorite vegetable?

★ Have you been eating a rainbow of fruits and vegetables?

Attach a Picture of Your Mosaic

PROTEIN & FAT

Supplies:
- ❏ Recipe and ingredients
- ❏ Storyboard
  - ❏ Paper
  - ❏ Markers or crayons or colored pencils or paint
- ❏ Stop motion
  - ❏ Video recorder
  - ❏ Prop materials: like clay or playdough or pencils or markers, etc.

Time to Complete: 1~2 Weeks

I grew up in an era that was afraid of eating anything with fat. Thankfully, I was not aware of that advice. My parents would buy half of a cow every year, to fill our freezer, and my dad would hunt for deer, elk and pheasants. That is what we would eat for most of our meals. I had no idea that the free-range deer, elk, and pheasant were so nutritious. Animals that are raised in their most natural state are the healthiest to eat! In fact, cows that are allowed to graze on fresh green grass actually have brain healthy omega 3 oils in their fats. Which means that those grass-fed cows produce healthy butters, creams, and beef products. When cows or other animals eat products with a lot of chemicals, many of those chemicals get stored away in the fat of those animals. Their bodies do not know how to process the unfamiliar man-made chemicals, which is why they are sent into their fat cells. So, when possible, it is a healthy choice to eat fats from organically fed animals. Sometimes that is not possible, they are still a good source of protein. If that is the case, it would be better to trim off the excess fats.

This is also true of eggs. Chickens that are allowed to scurry around eating worms and bugs, which are their natural diet, produce healthier eggs. Often the yolks are a much deeper orange color and contain more nutrients than chickens raised indoors being fed chicken meal.

Protein is very important for our bodies to grow and develop muscles. Proteins are made up of amino acids and it is very hard to get all the essential amino acids without eating protein.

Fats are really important for our brains and for every cell of our bodies. Cells are made of a phospholipid bilayer that is made of healthy fats. When we eat unhealthy fats, our brain and our cells suffer and we can become ill.

Examples of healthy proteins:

Chicken and Turkey
Pheasants
Salmon
Beef
Eggs
Elk
Deer

*If possible, choose free-range and
    organic protein sources and
    wild-caught fish.

Examples of healthy fats:

Grass-fed organic butter and
    cream
Coconut oil
Avocados and avocado oil
Olive Oil
Walnut oil

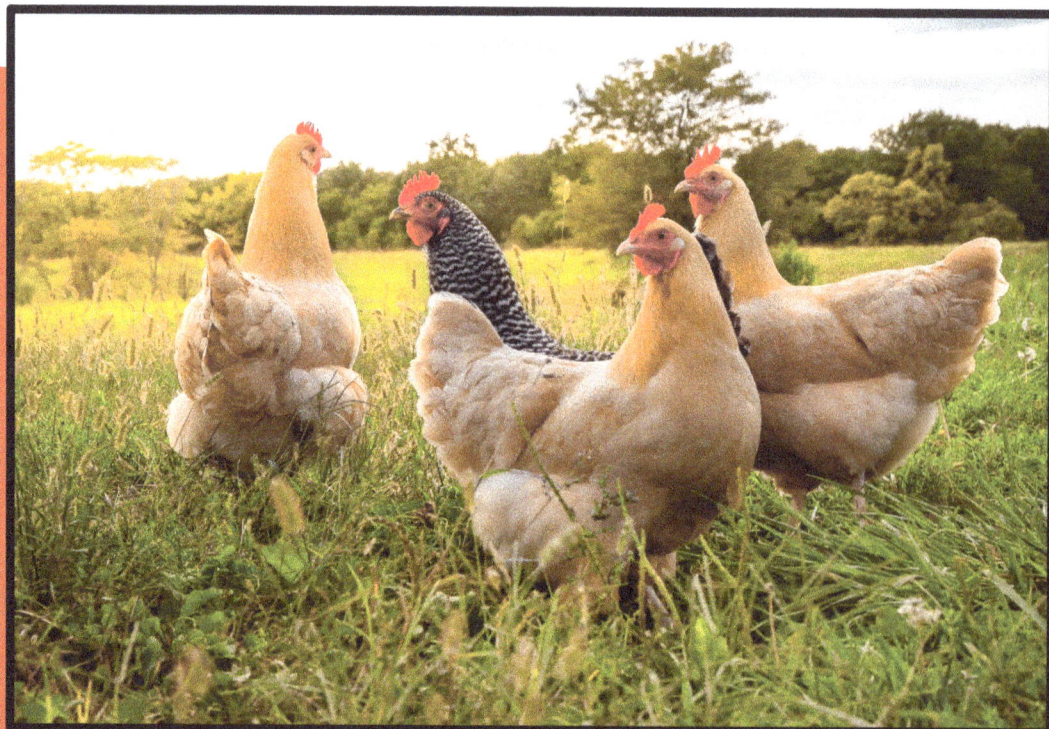

ACTIVITY

Find a recipe that uses good proteins and fats. Make that recipe with a family member or friend. Take a picture of your final product. To make your meal even healthier, include colorful vegetables and a tall glass of water. Set up the table with a beautiful display of healthy foods. Sit down with someone, appreciate the delicious food you are about to eat, and share a meal together. Write out your recipe below and attach a picture.

RECIPE

★ How did you feel sharing your healthy meal with someone?

PICTURE

★ Was it fun to make a meal?

★ How many different colors did you have in your meal?

★ What other meals would you like to learn to make?

ACTIVITY

Think about one of the following processes. Create a fictional character (representing one of the objects in the process) and write a fun story about that character. Be creative! Integrate what you have learned about proteins and/or fats and health. Feel free to do a little research to learn more about your topic.

- A salmon's journey from fresh water to the sea and back to fresh water
- The day in the life of a cow
- Rise and shine as a chicken
- An egg's journey from the coop to the kitchen
- From a baby avocado to a bowl of guacamole
- An amino acid grows up to be a muscle
- From grass to ice-cream to human brain cells

After you write the story choose one of the following visual activities to correlate with your story.

- Draw or design, with a computer, story panels with pictures
- Create a short video with pictures or use stop motion or claymation.
- Create a clay or playdough representation of your story.

ACTIVITY

Attach your story panels or a picture of your project below.

Share your story with someone. Make sure to tell them how important healthy proteins and fats are for your body!

★   What did you learn as you created your story?

Life of a Chicken

An empty nest.

A mother giving birth.

The start of a new life.

Cracking as the baby escapes to enter the new world.

Life of a Chicken

A baby chick leaving to explore the world for the first time.

Baby chicks must eat healthy worms to grow strong.

They need exercise too to live a healthy life.

They then grow to continue the life cycle.

SUGAR & SWEETS

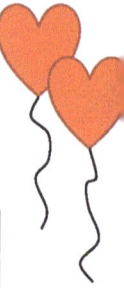

Supplies:	Time to Complete:
❑ Drama props	1~2 Weeks

As a child I was a very intuitive eater. If I was not hungry, then I did not eat, no matter what goodies were being served. I would save my Easter and Halloween candy until it was no longer good. If I had the choice of apple pie or an apple I would often pick the apple. This was not because I had a knowledge of what was healthier, but just because that is what I wanted. Maybe my body was telling me what would make it feel best. Over time I started to enjoy treats more and listened to my body less. Now that I am in my forties my body is reminding me of what it prefers and I am making choices based on what my mind knows is best. When I eat sugars I have bad joint pain, making it hard to walk or bend my knees and even my fingers. I am choosing the more natural treats because my body feels much better when I do. I still indulge once in a while, but the majority of the time I choose what makes me feel the best.

Foods that have a lot of refined sugars are extra work for our bodies. Our bloodstream is only supposed to have a narrow limit of sugars floating around and the body needs to shuttle the extra sugars out of the blood stream, using insulin, to remain in a healthy balance. When way too much sugar is in the bloodstream, from overeating on cookies, cakes, candy, etc., the body over responds to get it out quickly and our blood sugar levels drop lower than they should be. When they drop too low we crave more sugar to get them back up. Often we overcompensate and eat too much sugary food causing the levels to go too high and then the cycle starts all over again. You can see these two cycles in the graph below. The normal cycle is in the center represented by blue, blood sugar that is too high and too low is represented by red.

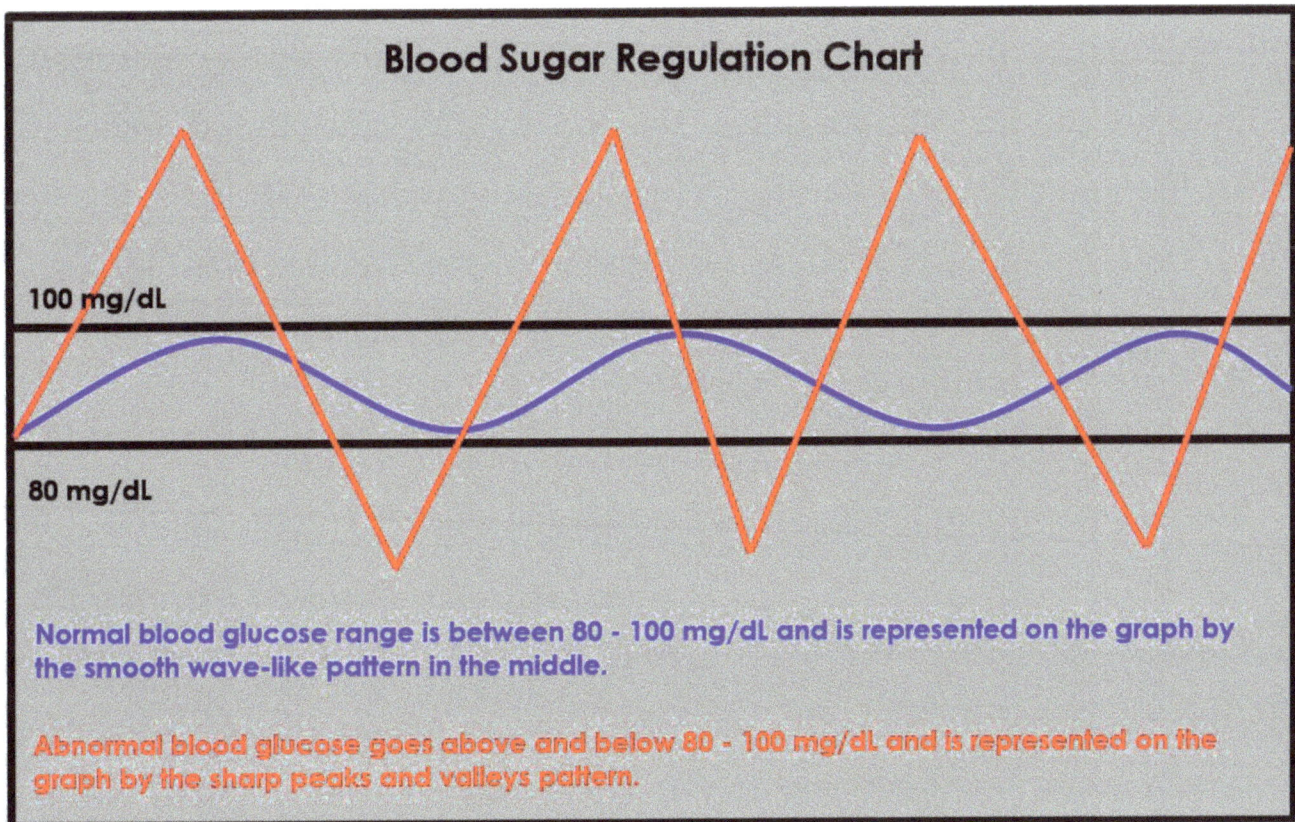

Blood Sugar Regulation Chart

100 mg/dL

80 mg/dL

Normal blood glucose range is between 80 - 100 mg/dL and is represented on the graph by the smooth wave-like pattern in the middle.

Abnormal blood glucose goes above and below 80 - 100 mg/dL and is represented on the graph by the sharp peaks and valleys pattern.

When people constantly overeat sugary foods, their bodies can become diabetic. Type II diabetes is a dangerous illness that can lead to heart disease, nerve damage, and more. My grandmother and great-grandmother both had type II diabetes. I remember them giving themselves shots on a daily basis. Due to the diabetes, my great-grandmother was blind by the time she died. I learned when I was young that staying healthy was important for me to help prevent becoming a type II diabetic.

Eating treats is something special that is associated with celebrations like birthdays and holidays. Unless you have a medical condition, these celebrations can still include treats. But, eating these sugary treats on a daily basis is not good for your health. Fortunately, there are ways to still enjoy treats without putting your health at risk. Fruits are nature's delicious treats. Not only are they sweet, they contain healthy nutrients like antioxidants. Fruit that is in-season and picked at its ripest point is so yummy! I love a bowl full of fresh berries with a little cream poured over the top.

★   What are your favorite healthy treats?

★   Does anyone in your family have a food-related illness?

★   Are there any sugary treats that you could substitute with a healthier option?

★   Do you notice feeling better when you eat healthier?

ACTIVITY

Create a drama, with your friends or siblings, based around blood-sugar regulation. Gather or make props to go along with your drama. Below are a few ideas, but feel free to make-up your own. If you need to, do a little more research about your topic to add more information to your drama.

Possible ideas:

- The interactions between insulin and blood sugar
- The life of a set of twins: one that leads a healthy life and the other that does not and is pre-diabetic
- The story of a group of kids that change their lives to be healthier
- A grandma sharing her experiences with her granddaughter

Practice your drama, then gather together your friends and family and share your performance.

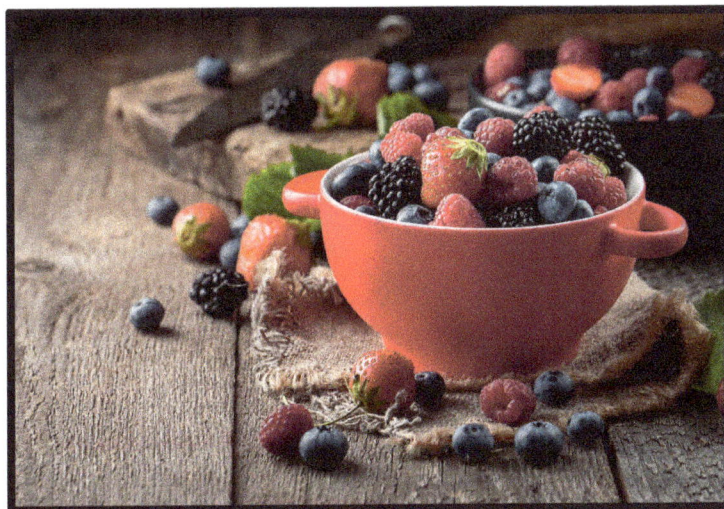

Describe your drama below

REFLECTION

★ What was your favorite part of your drama?

★ What was the reaction of the audience members?

★ What is your biggest take-away from this activity?

★ Reflect back to the last lesson. What proteins and fats have you eaten this past week?

MOVEMENT & SLEEP

Supplies:	Time to Complete:
❑ Favorite writing pen(s) ❑ Paper	1~2 Weeks

As I watch children they are always moving and doing. Toddlers never really walk, they run places. I cannot imagine how funny it would look if adults moved around like toddlers. Maybe that is part of the reason toddlers need naps. So they can rest up for their next running session. I have realized that when I have been sitting for a long period of time it is actually harder to get up and start moving than when I am already up. Often I will say to my children, "since you are already up, will you get me a glass of water?" It seems so silly, I have been sitting and should have more energy, but that is not how it works. I think of Newton's First Law of Motion that states that an object at rest stays at rest and an object in motion stays in motion, unless acted upon by another force. That is true for me.

While it is easier to stay sitting, that is not what is best for my body or brain. The longer we sit, the less oxygen our brains are receiving and the less efficient they are at learning and remembering. This is one of the disadvantages of sitting at school for long periods of time. Also, moving our bodies so that we are crossing the midline gets our blood flowing across the hemispheres of our brain. This allows us to learn and think better too. In fact, a brain-break is not a break from thinking, it is a break from sitting. When you have been working for a long period of time it is good for your brain and body to get up and move around for a while. You could dance, shake out your body, tap your body starting at your feet and work your way up your body, walk around, just do something physical. You will feel refreshed and your cells will be stimulated. You will be ready to tackle your mental project much better afterwards.

★   What is your favorite way to move?

★   How do you feel after moving?

If you are sitting much of your day, it might help if you set a timer to remind yourself to get up and move. That could also be a good time to drink some water.

★   Do you sit a lot during the day?

★   How could you move more during the day?

When you have pushed your body through hard-work, it feels great to sit down to relax or go to bed. You can feel a good tingling throughout your body knowing it has worked hard. This is also good for your muscles. The more you use your muscles, the stronger they will get. This is good for your health. Strong muscles help to support your body and protect it.

Lastly, it is very important for you to rest. You probably need more sleep than you realize. As your body is growing and developing, you need more sleep than adults, which is around seven to eight hours. It is good to think about what time you need to be up and make sure you get to bed early enough to get your rest. While you are resting your body is busy healing and building up your immune system and growing muscles. You will feel and function more optimally if you make sure to get your needed rest at night.

It helps to develop a routine. I have to wake up at 5 am. So, I need to be asleep by 9pm to get eight hours of sleep. I can not start getting ready for bed at 9 pm, I have to start earlier. So, I take my shower and get myself ready for bed so that I am in bed around 8:30-8:45 pm. That way I can read and relax before going to sleep.

★ Do you have a nightly routine to prepare you for a good night of sleep?

★ How much sleep do you get each night?

★ What time do you need to go to bed to get at least eight hours of sleep (remember, if you are younger you need more sleep, maybe nine or ten hours-listen to your parents and your body)?

ACTIVITY

Think about all the lessons we have gone through and write a song that includes all the areas. Then create dance moves to correlate with your song. Get a friend or two to join you and practice your song and dance. You can pick a popular song you like and change the words, this is called contrafactum. This is a great way to move your body, review what you have learned, and have fun. When you have your song and dance moves down, perform for someone. If you want, one person can sing and the others can dance or you could record your song and everyone could dance. It is up to you, this is your song.

Areas we have covered:

- Eating in a parasympathetic (calm, enjoyable, thankful) state
- Drinking enough water
- Eating colorful fruits and vegetables
- Eating good proteins and fats
- Substituting healthy sweets
- Movement and sleep

★ What is the name of your song?

★ If you changed the words to a popular song, what was it?

Write out the lyrics to your song

REFLECTION

★ Think back to all the lessons in this book. What activity was your favorite?

★ What have you learned throughout this activity guide?

★ What healthy changes have you made in your life?

Being healthy is a continual process. Like making your bed each day, you have to drink water everyday, choose colorful fruits and vegetables, eat proteins and fats that are body and brain building, swap out sugary desserts with better options (most of the time), move your body, and get enough sleep each night (there might be a few exceptions). By living healthy day-to-day, you are more likely to avoid many lifestyle diseases like type II diabetes and you will have a sharper brain and stronger body to do the things you want to do.

FINAL THOUGHTS

As you continue to grow in your journey, think about more ways you can add to your healthy habits. Some possible ideas are planting a garden, learning a new sport or activity, taking a cooking class, buying a healthy cookbook and cooking your way through it. You can also build on your creative side. If you enjoyed the watercolor painting, then look up how-to videos online and create more beautiful works of art or try other types of paint, there are many ways to write poetry, look up the different ways and create a book of your own poetry, you could even create your own book cover, if you like working with clay or playdough mold away, write more songs, create dances alone or with friends, become an amazing storyteller, make more mosaics to go along with the one you created, frame them and hang them on your wall. Using your brain and creating art is a healthy habit that also feeds the soul. Now that you have had an introduction to the many arts and healthy practices I wish you the best of luck at enhancing your life. I want you to go on to be the best you and to continue adding to your story, making it the story you want it to be. I hope these activities have been fun and in the process helped you to create habits that will enhance your health and life. ♥

Thank you to my dear husband David for all your support emotionally, physically, and financially as I have worked to complete my Functional Nutritional Therapy Certification, Master's degree, and this book project.

I also want to thank my four children, Alyse, Luke, Mark, and Michael for being my test subjects and practice students with all of my projects over the years.

Alyse, you have been a springboard for so many ideas, your help has been invaluable. Thank you for the storyboard and artwork.

Mark, thank you for the yummy popcorn balls.

Lastly, I would like to thank all my professors, teachers, and classmates for the lessons and laughter.

Shanda lives in Boise, Idaho. She is a secondary public school teacher and a certified functional nutritional therapist. She enjoys spending time with her husband and four children, as well as petting her two kitties, reading books about nutrition and education, cooking and baking, and soaking in the beautiful outdoors.

www.ingramcontent.com/pod-product-compliance
Lightning Source LLC
Chambersburg PA
CBHW040248100426
42811CB00011B/1192